Original title:
The Charm of Leather

Copyright © 2025 Creative Arts Management OÜ
All rights reserved.

Author: Charles Whitfield
ISBN HARDBACK: 978-1-80586-045-7
ISBN PAPERBACK: 978-1-80586-517-9

Touch of Grit

In a jacket that's seen some roads,
Zippers creak like ancient codes.
Pockets stuffed with treasures rare,
Lost buttons float like thoughts in air.

A belt that's worn, no style to brag,
Holds up pants that always sag.
A scuff here, a scratch right there,
Each mark tells tales of life's wild fare.

Emblems of the Past

This bag has lived through sun and rain,
A witness to shopping spree and gain.
Its corners frayed, a story spun,
From late-night snacks to morning fun.

A wallet bursting with old receipts,
Dates on slips like faded beats.
Memories tucked in every seam,
Each wallet holds a laughter's dream.

Curves of Utility

A pair of shoes, they squeak with pride,
Danced through puddles, ran and slide.
Laces untied, they always dare,
To trip and fall without a care.

A case for shades, it's been around,
Holding secrets without a sound.
It's been squashed in bags, tossed in the back,
But springs back fresh, not one thing it lacks.

Embracing the Elements

A coat defying wind and chill,
With pockets deep, it fits the bill.
It's got a tear but don't you fret,
It flaps with flair, a fashion pet.

Gloves that grip, not one size right,
A mismatch dance in evening light.
Through rain and gusts, they laugh and shout,
Who needs perfection when fun's about?

Aged Allure

Old jacket with tales to tell,
Worn by a dancer who fell.
With every crack, a giggle grows,
Fashion faux pas? Who really knows?

Stains of coffee, a badge of pride,
Comfort in chaos, nowhere to hide.
Each fold a secret, each tear a laugh,
Outdated? No! It's a fashion gaffe!

Heartbeats of Humanity

A belt that knows my waist too well,
Holds up my pants and my tales to tell.
In every loop, a laugh resides,
Like buddies on a wild ride.

Soft as butter, tough as nails,
It squeaks when I tell goofy tales.
Every creak a chuckle shared,
This trusty hide has always cared.

Journey in Each Stitch

Each stitch is like a funny punchline,
Quilting joy in leather divine.
My wallet holds more than just cash,
Memories brimming, in a flash!

Threads of laughter, colors bright,
Flaps of joy take joyful flight.
Every snap, a silly dance,
Crafting smiles, our sweet romance.

Canvas of Comfort

The sofa, a hug in disguise,
With cushions that have seen all our lies.
A luxury seat for midnight snacks,
Even the cat seems to relax.

In crinkles and creases, stories dwell,
Of spills and thrills, and the time I fell.
This cozy spot where laughter blooms,
In a world of chaos, it brightens rooms.

Palette of Shadows

In a world of stitched together plays,
A sofa's got more stories than delays.
It swallows up the couch potato's sighs,
With every dent, a tale that never dies.

Bags that squawk and squeak like a hen,
Chasing down memories again and again.
They sit on shelves, a proud display,
With dusty laughs, they flirt and sway.

Coated in History

On dusty racks where treasures lie,
A mouse in boots would surely sigh.
With each crack and crease, it shimmies and shakes,
Pondering all the crumbs it makes.

Chairs that creak like a wise old sage,
Don't mind the spills; they're part of the page.
Each mark a memoir of wild nights out,
Where cocktails sang and laughter sprouted.

Narratives in Notches

Scuffs tell tales of clumsy falls,
While cats have claimed their throne on the walls.
Each notch a laugh, each scratch a cheer,
Reminding us of all we hold dear.

Couches double as dance floors at night,
With unwelcome guests taking flight.
They may seem old, but oh, what flair!
With a wink and a nudge, they've seen it all there.

Harmony of Hues

From charred to bright, a swirling dance,
A leather feast that enchants at a glance.
Bright colors argue, then settle down,
Like bickering siblings sporting a frown.

Light shades giggle, dark tones pout,
In this madcap world, there's no doubt.
They shuffle together, a jolly crew,
Bringing quirks to life—who knew?

Tales Stitched in Memory

In a shop where wallets prance,
Old shoes tell their vibrant dance.
Each stitch a tale of wild delight,
Bouncing leather under moonlight.

A jacket's laugh, a belt's sly grin,
Sitting proud, they tease the skin.
They've survived spills and some fierce play,
With every scratch, they scream, "Hooray!"

Patina of Lost Journeys

A bag that's traveled near and far,
Holds secrets like a wishing star.
From dusty roads to rainy skies,
Its creases whisper, full of lies.

With every wrinkle, tales unfold,
Of misadventures brave and bold.
Each mark a laugh, a stumble, a cheer,
The journey's fun, let's grab a beer!

Caress of a Forgotten Embrace

A couch that hugs with leather arms,
That holds the giggles, the charms,
Of quiet nights and popcorn fights,
It's a throne for dreams, with no heights.

With cushions soft as laughter flows,
In creased valleys, humor grows.
It may have aged, but still it beams,
A couch that loves, or so it seems!

Shadows of Rustic Market Stalls

In stalls where craftsmanship does play,
Prices drop, hairdresser's sway.
Leather items winking bright,
Packaged dreams caught in nightlight.

A wallet sings, a purse does sway,
Bartering with a smile each day.
With every deal, a joke is spun,
In this market, laughter's won!

Dance of the Tanned

In the closet, jackets twirl,
They've got moves that make you swirl.
With zippers clicking, and buttons bright,
They boogie down all day and night.

A pair of shoes just can't resist,
They're tapping toes, they can't be missed.
With every step, they sing a tune,
While belts play trumpet under the moon.

Each flap and crevice has a tale,
Of dancing nights and drinks that sail.
Oh, how they jiggle, laugh, and glide,
In this odd fashion show, they take pride!

For every fold and every seam,
Is wrapped in joy—a leather dream!
So slip into your party gear,
And join the dance, my dear, my dear!

The Scent of Ripe Memories

Fragrant whiffs from jackets past,
Take me back to joys that last.
The smell of mischief, laughter loud,
Through every fold, adventures proud.

Saddles creak like ancient bones,
Each sniff brings back the silly tones.
Chasing friends and missing socks,
Pooling memories in old docks.

Handbags whisper of treasure maps,
And dance with ripples, giggles, claps.
They tell of secrets, sly and bold,
Wrapped in stories from days of old.

So when you smell that weathered charm,
Remember joy does have its arm.
With every inhale, take a trip,
To where our dusty dreams still skip!

Veins of Vintage

In the texture lies a rustic flair,
Each scratch and scuff has stories to share.
Oh, the thrill of finding a gem,
A treasure chest, where tales stem!

Old wallets crinkle with pocket change,
Pledging love in a world so strange.
They hide receipts of meals unpaid,
And secrets in the folds—handmade!

Hats with brims that capture rain,
Sipping sunlight without disdain.
They've seen the dawn of many days,
With tipsy tales in playful ways.

So let's toast to vintage and flair,
In every crease, joy's sitting there.
With laughter echoing, it's plain to see,
The treasures of life's grand jubilee!

Patina of Passion

A jacket worn and lovingly frayed,
Each nick and mark, a memory played.
With patches claiming heart and glee,
Like stickers on a bear—oh, what a spree!

The belt that hugs with quite the flair,
Whispers secrets, if you dare.
It holds together things we wear,
While laughing at our bold affair.

Shoes that stumble in rhythm's chase,
With playful scuffs that set the pace.
Who knew a sole could dance like this?
A playful twirl, a misstep bliss!

So raise a toast to all we've worn,
Each leather heart a little worn.
With every scratch, there's joy inside,
In this wild ride—let's take the stride!

Essence of Existence

In a world so slick and fine,
A jacket dances, looking divine.
It's got tales stitched in its seams,
Whispers of dreams, in laughter it beams.

A wallet grins, snug in your back,
Its secrets safe, never in a crack.
With coins it jingles, a merry sound,
A treasure trove by fun's abound.

Shoes that squeak with every step,
They shimmy and shake, what a pep!
Each scuff a story, a witty line,
Your feet are laughing, feeling fine!

Oh what a life with leather wear,
It lives and breathes, with such flair.
Chasing whims, we twirl and prance,
In the embrace of fun's wild dance.

Documented in Darts

In the corner of a smoky bar,
A leather vest boasts tales bizarre.
With darts it dances, takes its aim,
Hitting the bullseye, a game of fame.

Belts that hold up more than pants,
With every buckle, they do their dance.
They whisper secrets of wild nights,
In the glow of neon, laughter ignites.

A bag that bounces, full of charms,
Holds memories in its loving arms.
It chuckles softly, a loyal friend,
With stories shared, it'll never end.

In the fabric of fun, they are entwined,
A raucous journey, humor designed.
With each laugh and every pout,
Leather's the life, that's what it's about.

Guardians of the Grit

Shoe soles tell of journeys grand,
With scuffed edges, they take a stand.
Through puddles and paths, they trot with glee,
Guardians of grit, just wild and free!

Jackets swagger, holding their ground,
As if to say, 'Look at me, I'm profound!'
With zippers that glimmer, they catch the light,
Daring the world, to dance through the night.

Purses wittily winking their eyes,
Sassy and bold, what a surprise!
They cradle trinkets, laughter inside,
In the shenanigans, they take pride.

So raise a toast to the leather brigade,
With goofy grins, let's dance unafraid.
For every scuff tells a tale to be told,
In this laugh-filled life, let's be bold!

Aurora in Aging

With creases that tell of the years gone by,
A leather couch gives a whoosh and sigh.
It wears its wisdom like a crown,
Whispering tales of the ups and downs.

Old shoes shuffle with stories to share,
Worn but cozy, they give a flair.
Each squeak is a chuckle, each step a cheer,
In the embrace of time, they persevere.

Jackets fade but their charm stays bright,
Like a well-loved cuddle on a chilly night.
They laugh at the wrinkles, dance with the dust,
For in every flaw, there's a sprinkle of trust.

So here's to the ages, the leather and fun,
Life's a wild ride, but oh, what a run!
Embracing the laughter in every crease,
In the beauty of aging, we find our peace.

Craft of the Age

In crafting hides with joy and glee,
A jacket stitched is plain to see.
With every poke and every seam,
We fashion dreams, or so we dream.

A wallet here, a belt that's sly,
Can hold your cash and let it fly.
Oh, fingers sore and threads that fray,
But look at what we've made today!

With polish bright and shine so bold,
A pair of boots, a tale retold.
When squirrels stare with jealous eyes,
We strut around, the world our prize.

So let us toast to wallets wide,
To leather goods we cannot hide.
In every stitch, some mischief's stored,
With each design, a laugh restored.

Kinship in the Fold

Have you met my friend, the purse?
With pockets deep, it's quite diverse.
At parties, he always steals the show,
And when he winks, oh what a glow!

A sofa here, a chair that sways,
In every fold, we laugh and play.
We share our secrets, stories old,
In leather's warmth, we're brave and bold.

With sleeves of cocoa, pants of brown,
We dance together, up and down.
In hand-me-downs or brand new threads,
We sport our pride, no room for dreads.

So gather round, my leather kin,
Let's share some jokes and guffaws within.
For every stitch is woven tight,
In this grand fold, our hearts take flight.

Timeless Embrace

When I slipped on that jacket snug,
I felt a warmth, a cozy hug.
It laughed at me with every groove,
A timeless laugh that makes me move.

Oh, leather boots, they stomp and tap,
With every step, they are the map.
Through puddles deep and mud so thick,
I waddle home and think it's slick.

A satchel bold, it guards my snacks,
A treasure chest that never lacks.
In markets bright, we strut and sway,
This timeless style, come what may.

So here's to hides in every place,
With quirky charms, they set the pace.
In every fold, a giggle waits,
A life embraced, that's how it rates.

North Star of Fashion

Oh look, there shines a belt so fine,
It cinches doubts, it draws the line.
With buckles bright and colors grand,
A guiding star for every hand.

With leather hats that twist and twirl,
We spark the streets and give a whirl.
The fashion police may swoop on through,
But watch us dance, we'll break the blue!

A cushion soft and shoes that squeak,
They tap and giggle, too much cheek!
Each step creates a laughter stream,
As leather sings the fashion theme.

So wear it proud, this playful skin,
In every laugh, let life begin.
North stars twinkle, style shall sway,
A funny twist in each array.

A Canvas of Human Experiences

In a store where the wallets play,
I found a purse that's quite the prey.
With every zip, it made a sound,
Like a piglet oinking in the ground.

Bags that wink, jackets that tease,
Worn-out shoes, oh, what a breeze!
The squeaks and creaks of every thread,
Talk back to me like a wise old head.

Belts that claim to hold it all,
But when I eat, they start to brawl.
A coat that hugs me way too tight,
Snickers laugh at my fashion plight.

Each item here has tales to tell,
Of laughs and spills, and oh, quite swell!
In this bazaar of silly dreams,
I'm lost in a maze of leather schemes.

Memories Forged in Fading Light

My jacket's seen more than a shoe,
It danced through life, oh what a view!
In bars, parties, and pizza runs,
It might just be the best of puns.

A briefcase full of 'important' stuff,
But really, it's just a snack stash, tough!
Crumpled receipts, old gum and a pen,
Who knew it was a treasure den?

Shoes that squeal when I walk on air,
They've got the rhythm, without a care.
With every step, they hum a tune,
A melody to make the grumpies swoon.

A backpack packed with stories rare,
Of jelly spills and one-eyed stares,
Remembered echoes fill the night,
As laughter dances in fading light.

Whispers of Worn Edges

My wallet whispers secrets clear,
Of coffee spills and many a beer.
It creaks and groans as I pay the fee,
Saying, 'Please, just let me be free!'

A belt that tries to hold my waist,
But with each meal, it's a race!
I hear it mutter 'not again',
But at the buffet, I'm a ten out of ten!

The couch where I lost a pen,
And found some snacks I forgot again.
Each cushion holds its own delight,
In a world where crumbs take flight.

I wear my stories like a crown,
With zippers that moan and buttons down.
In every crease, there's laughter seen,
In this life, I reign supreme!

Texture of Timelessness

A lovely bag that's lost its snap,
But still it bravely holds my map.
Each worn patch tells of travels grand,
Through artful streets and food stands.

My shoes are old, but full of flair,
They stomp around and shake the air.
With laces frayed and colors bright,
They jiggle with joy in morning light.

A jacket that's been through every fall,
It's more than threads; it's memories, all!
With every tear, a laugh emerges,
As stitching tells of life's converges.

In this dance of fabric and time,
It's a riddle wrapped up in rhyme.
For in each style and every seam,
Lies a heartbeat, a living dream.

Sirens of Studio

In the studio there's a smell,
Of polished hide, oh what a swell!
Stitching away with threads of gold,
Creating tales that never grow old.

A jacket winked, said, 'Take me out!'
A quirky hat just wants to shout.
Sassy shoes with a cheeky flair,
They trip on toes, not a single care.

Belts are slung with flair and sass,
Each buckle shines like party glass.
With every snap, a little tease,
These pieces dance, they aim to please.

So let's make fun of this fine craft,
With every stitch, a master's laugh.
In this realm of leather wear,
Life's a joke, but oh, we care!

Unearthed Elegance

Among the piles of dusty finds,
A jacket waits with elegant lines.
'Polish me and take a chance!'
It winks and thrums a dapper dance.

A purse with style, it sways and twirls,
Singing songs of fitting girls.
'Fill me with secrets, tales of fun!'
It giggles softly, a charm undone.

Boots with attitude, laced so tight,
They strut around like stars at night.
Each step a stomp, a laugh, a cheer,
In this ballroom of leather, they grace the year.

The elegance is full of jokes,
With every stitch, it gently pokes.
Let's raise a toast to our fine finds,
Unearthed treasures, our hearts entwined!

Reverberations of Touch

A gentle tap on leather's skin,
A sound that dances, pulls you in.
Every crease a quirky beat,
It thumps and booms beneath your feet.

'Feel my texture!' a bag will sing,
While jackets sway, their praises ring.
Softly they giggle with every stroke,
In the hands of jokers, they provoke.

A patchwork seat will sway and sway,
It knows the jokes, it knows the play.
Lounging about, it takes a rest,
Who knew that leather is so blessed?

So let's applaud this wondrous feel,
With laughter stitched, it's oh so real.
In every touch, a story lies,
In reverberations, the laughter flies!

Character in Crinkles

Oh, look at those delightful folds,
Each wrinkle hides a story told.
A moment's mishap, a spilled drink,
Can turn a leather seat to winks.

A couch with creases, pleats galore,
Whispers secrets, never a bore.
'Take a seat!' it grins with glee,
As pillows bounce like a bumblebee.

A handbag crinkled, full of cheer,
It jests, 'I've held too much beer!'
With zippers that giggle and clink,
In a world of leather, life's a wink.

So celebrate each curvy line,
In every crinkle, we see the shine.
Life's messy? Oh, that's the trick,
With character in crinkles, we'll always click!

Essence of Endurance

In a jacket worn, tales collide,
Stains and scuffs, a source of pride.
With every scratch, a funny tale,
Adventures lost, yet never pale.

The couch, a throne, now slightly bent,
Where pizza crumbs become content.
Each fold recalls a wild old dance,
Where humor grew, not from romance.

A belt that's seen a dozen diets,
Promises made, but none that try it.
With every poke, it jesters loud,
While jeans just laugh, quite unbowed.

So here's to leather, quirks embrace,
With every wrinkle, a smiling face.
The stories weave, a life that's cheer,
In cracks and creases, we hold dear.

Erosion of Elegance

A handbag once meant for the chic,
Now holds receipts, it's gone antique.
With lipstick stains and crumbs galore,
A fashionista's laugh, not a bore.

The shoes that once danced through the night,
Now squeak and creak, a funny sight.
Each step a chuckle, each scuff a grin,
As elegance slips, let fun begin.

The gloves that fit like a second skin,
Now stretch and bend with laughter thin.
A friend to warmth, with quirks and flaws,
Their charm's in how they break the laws.

So toast to it, this leather wear,
With all its quirks, we stop and stare.
For in this mess, elegance hides,
A humorous tale where laughter rides.

Robust Romance

Oh the wallet, thick as a book,
Love letters tucked in, take a look.
Each credit card tells a romance fine,
While receipts crumple, like lost valentine.

The sofa squeaks with tales of fun,
Where popcorn fights unite as one.
In cozy nights, the cushions tease,
As laughter echoes with gentle ease.

A belt that binds, yet sets us free,
With holes like memories, can't you see?
Each loop a laugh, each notch a cheer,
When love wears leather, joy comes near.

So let us dance with this bold embrace,
For in each scrape, passion finds place.
In rugged realms, romance so bright,
Laughing through life, feels just right.

Symphonies of Strength

The boots that stomp through puddles wild,
Collecting mud, like a playful child.
They march with pride, a clumsy beat,
In every puddle, laughter's sweet.

With jackets that hug like an old best friend,
Worn down seams, but never an end.
Each zipper stuck, a comic plight,
But oh! The strength in every fight.

A hat that's lost its shape and form,
Yet holds the warmth, defies the storm.
Its faded brim tells stories old,
With each new wearing, a joy untold.

So here's to leather, sturdy, bold,
In every sag, new laughs unfold.
With each odd quirk, we find our song,
In these symphonies, we all belong.

The Dance of Hide and Thread

In a workshop, tools all gleam,
A leather hide, a crafter's dream.
With thread in hand, they twist and twine,
Creating shapes, both strange and fine.

A belt that squeaks, a purse that grins,
In every fold, a tale begins.
The dye may run, the seams may fray,
But oh, the joy of the DIY play!

Crafting boots that dance with flair,
Each step a laugh, a jig, a dare.
With every stitch, a story's spun,
Of leather dreams and crafty fun!

In every fold, a quirk resides,
With mismatched bits and crafty guides.
So come and join this jolly band,
Where laughter reigns, and fun is planned.

Echoes of a Wanderer's Pack

Upon my back, a pack so stout,
It's filled with goodies, there's no doubt.
Crunchy snacks and maps askew,
A wanderer's life, all morning dew.

Each zip and snap, a rhythm sweet,
It bounces along with two-left feet.
From city streets to mountain highs,
It carries tales that never die.

A patch or two, a coffee stain,
Each scuff a laugh, each tear a gain.
As I roam far, it lets me be,
My trusty friend on this folly spree!

The weight of memories fills it up,
With every laugh, a sip, a cup.
So here's to packs, both old and bold,
Echoing stories yet untold.

Emblems of Strength and Grace

In the corner sits a chair quite grand,
With leather arms that truly stand.
It creaks and sighs when I take a seat,
A throne of comfort, oh what a treat!

Patina shines with every scratch,
A testament to time's own match.
Through spills and thrills, it holds its place,
An emblem worn with style and grace.

The old boots in the hallway stand,
With stories etched, not quite so planned.
They've leaped through puddles, danced on stone,
A testament to adventures known.

So let us toast to that worn chap,
With every scuff, a hearty clap.
For strength and grace in wear and tear,
Are stitched with love in every pair.

Aged Beauty and Bitter Sweetness

There's beauty here in lines and tears,
Old bags that tell of bygone years.
Each wrinkle hides a laugh or sigh,
A bittersweet farewell, oh my!

The once-bright color fades away,
But wisdom grows with every fray.
Aged leather speaks in whispers low,
Of laughter shared and friends we know.

In every scratch, a journey lived,
A romance penned, a heart once sieved.
With bittersweet in every fold,
A tapestry of tales retold.

So here's to leather, old yet fine,
With character that's purely divine.
For age brings charm, a wink, a glance,
In every piece, a sweet romance.

Silent Stories

In the corner, a jacket waits,
Its pockets whisper of secret dates.
Shoes that squeak like curious cats,
Tell tales of wanderings, you know, like that!

Couches where mischief took its seat,
Each scratch and scuff a sign of heat.
A belt that's seen a dance or two,
Who knew it could do the twist with you?

Wallets with laughter, spills, and change,
Adventures that felt a bit strange.
Handbags heavy with stories old,
Trying to keep their secrets bold.

So here's to the leather, both brave and mild,
With every wear, it's just like a child.
It laughs and plays, oh what a show,
In its silent stories, watch how they glow!

Quests of Quality

Once a boot set out on a quest,
To find the comfiest place to rest.
But in puddles, it took a dive,
And emerged with a smile, so alive!

A bag declared, 'I'm made for fun!'
'Take me out, let's run and run!'
But it tripped on the curb, oh dear!
Yet laughed it off without a fear.

Belts, they boast of strength and flair,
Holding up tales of flair and scare.
One cheeky strap said with a wink,
'At least I hold everything, don't overthink!'

And thus the leather, on quests they roam,
With every mishap, they find a home.
Full of laughter, quirks, and splendid cheer,
Who knew they carried such stories here?

Entrances to Enigma

An old suitcase, dusty yet spry,
Holds mysteries under its lid, oh my!
What did it see through the years it spent?
Were they wild parties or a quiet event?

A satchel grins with secrets to share,
Of shady deals or a friendly dare.
With pockets that hold a candy or two,
Every journey leads back to you.

A leather patch on the couch, so bold,
Knows the stories it's silently told.
Did it host a snore or a midnight snack?
With cushions tall, it's got no lack.

These entrances tease with puzzles so grand,
Of leather's mishaps in our quirky land.
With every scuff, a tale does appear,
In the enigma of leather, there's joy, never fear!

Tactile Treasures

In a world of fabric, soft and sleek,
The fibers often squeak and peak.
But there's a texture that steals the show,
It's like a hug from an old hippo, yo!

When I wear my jacket, it's meant for flair,
I strut around with quite the air.
Bumps and creases, oh what a sight!
Is it fashion? Or just a... fright?

A bag that squeaks, a shoe that squeals,
All my friends laugh at my odd deals.
Yet as I prance, they can't help but grin,
Because who cares when you look this thin?

So here's to the stuff that loves to cling,
Making us feel like a zany king.
It may be quirky, but I must confess,
These tactile treasures beat the rest!

Pathways of the Grain

Every scratch tells a story, each line a laugh,
Like a toasty banana split on a collage path.
With textures from animals that once roamed free,
Who knew a wallet could hold such glee?

Strutting in boots that creak with style,
I stumble a lot, but hey, it's worthwhile!
Each step a journey, each slip a cheer,
Falling with grace, with a giggle and beer.

Pockets bursting, buttons flying,
My leather satchel? It's always trying.
To carry my snacks and my dreams alike,
Beans and wisdom, it's truly a hike.

So raise your mugs to every layer,
To the funny slips and the odd displayer.
For life is a dance on a supple stage,
With grains of laughter for every page.

Jewels of the Journey

A belt that's cracked, a wallet that squeals,
Worn and weathered, both boast their feels.
In the sunlit park, I strut so proud,
With snacks in my pockets, I'm humorously loud!

Each charm tells tales, and oh what a scene,
With every odd fold, it's a quirky routine.
If my trousers do sag, or my bag gives a sigh,
I just laugh it off, let the good times fly!

Sometimes I wonder where I went wrong,
When my footwear starts dancing to its own song.
But who needs perfect when fun is the goal?
I'll jive with my treasures, that's how I roll!

So here's to the journeys, with every dent,
To the goofy moments that life's really meant.
For in a world of fabric, soft and neat,
These jewels of the journey can't be beat!

Armor of Artisans

In my battle gear, I'm ready to fight,
With a jacket that squeaks like it's got some fright.
Crafted with care by hands skilled and grand,
Every stitch a chuckle, how odd it can stand!

I slide into shoes that have stories to share,
My toes can feel freedom, that's quite the affair.
And with each little scuff, I feel tougher and spry,
Like an ancient knight but I'm no good at pie!

Bags filled with snacks sprawl everywhere,
And my quirky attire elicits a stare.
But I stand with pride, just a laugh on my chest,
For all these odd treasures, I feel truly blessed!

So here's to the artisans, quirky and rare,
Creating our armors with personal flair.
With a chuckle and grin, I gladly parade,
For life's a grand adventure, I'm ready to wade!

Journeys Bound in Rich Texture

In pockets deep, a candy stash,
With every step, the leather cracks.
A purse that talks, oh what a thrill,
Shoes that squeak, add to the chill.

With every trip, there's tales to tell,
Of scuffs and stains, all is well.
Bouncing hats, and coats that twirl,
Each fold has secrets, ready to unfurl.

Tanned by sun, rain, and storm,
Like old friends, they keep you warm.
In each warp, a giggle stored,
As life unfolds, leather adored.

But beware the bumpy ride,
For a bag that's stout can be your guide.
With laughter stitched in every seam,
On this journey, we will gleam.

The Spirit of the Artisan's Touch

Created with care, a crafty whim,
Stitched and re-stitched, the edges slim.
A belt that's wider than my waist,
Coming loose; oh what a haste!

With buttons gleaming, colors bright,
Each piece a dance, a sheer delight.
A wallet chatters when it's full,
Like gossip spread, it's quite the pull.

In workshops live a playful crew,
Whose laughter pings when they construe.
A shoe that squeaks with every trot,
Bringing smiles, like jelly shots!

So here's to those who craft with glee,
Each item's joy, so wild and free.
With playful quirks and silly styles,
The spirit lives amidst the smiles.

Warmth of a Beloved Coat

Old coat, you whisper, tales of yore,
Worn with love, patched at the core.
In your pockets, candies hide,
And silly notes from the wild ride.

With every button, a story waits,
Laugh lines deepen with gentle fates.
A hood to hide, when times are rough,
Oh coat, you fit me like a glove.

Breath of warmth on crisp cold days,
You dance with shadows, in clever ways.
Through puddles splashing, and laughter flowing,
Your leather arms keep joy growing.

Yet when the rain trickles, oh dear,
You drip and droop, I shake in fear.
But with a chuckle, we brave the night,
With you beside, all's just alright.

Charisma in Creases and Cracks

See those lines, they tell a joke,
A bag that laughs, a quirky poke.
Each wrinkle sings of fun-filled days,
Bound together in joyful ways.

Sassy boots that strut and glide,
With squeaks that follow, side by side.
Leather stops and ponders near,
What wonder brings the world right here?

With a twist and turn, the seams all cheer,
Oh what charm, it feels so clear.
Repurposed scraps, a funky hat,
Each piece proud, imagine that!

So when you see those tiny flaws,
Think of the stories, give a pause.
In every crease, a giggle's packed,
The world's parade in fun's abstract.

Threads of Resilience

In a shop where odd things wait,
A jacket hid its secret fate.
With every stitch and every seam,
It bellowed out a silly dream.

A belt that cracks when you sit down,
Sports a leather grin, not a frown.
Around the waist it did a dance,
Claiming it's got style by chance!

Purses full of stories old,
Handling chaos, brave and bold.
With zippers that jingle like a clown,
They hoard our treasures, upside down.

So treasure threads with quirks so bright,
For life in leather can be a delight!
With every mark, a tale to tell,
Of resilience wrapped in a funny shell.

Beauty in Imperfection

A scuff here, a scratch there,
A handbag wears its past with flair.
Each little flaw's a badge of cheer,
Whispering tales that we hold dear.

A sandal squeaks like a silly tune,
Dancing under the bright full moon.
Look closer, and you'll surely see,
Imperfections make it uniquely free!

The wallet that has seen better days,
Still carries cash in stubborn ways.
It's cracked but holds those bills just right,
A fellow traveler, never uptight.

So let's applaud each dent and line,
For even chaos can seem divine.
In the world of leather, come what may,
Flaws spark joy in a quirky way.

Shadows of a Forged Life

In shadows cast by a cracked old chair,
Lies a story that floats in the air.
With every creak and every bend,
A raucous laughter with every friend.

Boots who've stomped through mud and rain,
Came home with tales of glorious pain.
They squeak with pride as they tell their lore,
Of dance floors skipped and grocery store.

A sofa that's soft yet bears a spot,
Is a throne of comfort, believe it or not!
Sit down, relax in its quirky embrace,
In the shadows of laughter, we find our place.

So raise a toast to the marks of fate,
For each old leather piece can lubricate.
With shadows trailing like a wise old sage,
They've danced through life, turning a page.

Caress of an Old Friend

An old jacket hugs you like a song,
Dancing along where memories belong.
With pockets full of secrets sweet,
It whispers funny tales on repeat.

A cap that's faded in sun and rain,
Holds tight to humor, never in vain.
Every bit of wear is a cheers and a grin,
For old friends rub off dust and sin.

A bag that drags a bit on the ground,
Hopes to gather laughter all around.
With every wobble and every flip,
It's riding life on a comedic trip.

So cherish what's worn, what's loved, what's real,
In every crease, find joy to feel.
For in the dance of leather so grand,
Lies the warmth of an old friend's hand.

Leathered Lullaby

In a coat that's seen some flair,
Cracks and creaks, a love affair.
The smell of history fills the air,
A hug from grandma? Not quite there!

Pockets deep, they hide a snack,
Spare gum, a lost kid's track.
With every scrape, there's a story,
Of epic fails wrapped in glory!

A belt that's thick, a fashion crime,
Holds your pants, but can't stand time.
Zip it up, or let it sag,
This style's tricky, don't you brag!

With stitches frayed and patches bold,
Each mark a tale, a secret told.
Wear it proud, let laughter bloom,
For every wrinkle holds a room!

Odyssey in Every Scrape

In a bag that's traveled far and wide,
Old maps of snacks and things we hide.
Each little scratch, a badge of pride,
A quest for chips? Oh, what a ride!

Shoes that squeak with every step,
Each footfall echoes like a pep.
Dancing in puddles, avoiding the mud,
Those leather boots? A splashy dud!

Jacket snug, it hugs too tight,
Hoping it won't start a fight.
With every bend, it screams for care,
This romance is a leather affair!

Layers worn, rugged and rugged,
With each adventure, a little snugged.
So when you trip, just take a grieve,
At least your style gives quite the weave!

Rustic Reveries

In a chair that creaks with age,
A leather seat, the perfect stage.
It swallows you whole, like a hug gone wrong,
And yet here we are, singing our song!

Looking for treasures in a wallet worn,
Coins and notes, oh how they're torn.
With every rustle, a wealth of flab,
Is that a receipt or a treasure map?

A suitcase that won't even close,
Filled with dreams and every pose.
Its zipper struggles — oh what a sight,
Packing your life? It's always a fight!

Mismatched gloves, one lost in haste,
In a fashion show that's gone to waste.
But if it fits, wear it with pride,
Worn and tattered? Just enjoy the ride!

Rituals of the Rough

Every morning, the leather calls,
With a creak and cracks, it softly brawls.
The dance of zippers, a morning show,
With every fasten, the cycle's flow!

Belt loops struggle, a tug of war,
"Where's the hole?" — it's humor galore!
Like a game of hide and seek, so bright,
Fashion dilemmas in morning light!

Polish or scuffs? The battle is real,
Shiny or matte, what's the deal?
Despite the wear, you'll look divine,
With every choice, the leather shines!

At the end of the day, let it rest,
Back on the hook, it's been truly blessed.
A ritual shared, a pact of trust,
In leather we live, in laughter we bust!

Secrets Held in Grain

Old jackets speak of nights,
With secrets tucked inside seams.
A pocket holds a snack or two,
And maybe quite a few dreams.

A wallet's tales of cash long gone,
Receipts like memories of past.
The grains of leather, soft and worn,
Keep stories deep and laughs amassed.

Each scuff and scratch a funny tale,
Of spills and laughter from all sides.
Unhad but cherished as you wear,
A grin that never quite hides.

So here's to leather, plush and tight,
A silly friend that won't let go.
With every twist in weaving tales,
It spins another tale of woe.

Luster Beneath Starlit Skies

Underneath the moon's bright gaze,
Jackets shimmer, a gleaming show.
They dance and sway like stars in flight,
Who knew they had such charm, oh who?

Each evening promises new fun,
With leather throngs and lively hearts.
The crackles of the night unfold,
As jackets squeak like laughing farts.

Slip into one and feel the thrill,
It's like a hug that's far too tight.
You can't help but break into grins,
As styles combine in pure delight.

So raise a toast to darkness near,
For leather dreams shoot high and free.
Under starlit laughter's reign,
We find our quirky jubilee.

Softness of Old Dreams

Soft dreams wrapped in vintage flair,
A sofa where the cat once sprawled.
When life was simple, nothing rare,
With laughter and joy that never stalled.

These old threads hold a gentle charm,
A couch that's seen a thousand shows.
And every crease tells tales of warmth,
Of quirky friends sharing highs and lows.

Cushions sigh as tales unwind,
Stories woven in each fold.
With every sit, a joy is mined,
As whispers of the past are told.

So here's to leather, stout and bright,
A conduit of whimsy years.
In every scratch, a laugh ignites,
A living book of joyful cheers.

Threads of Timeless Craft

With every stitch, a joke unfolds,
A craft that tickles and delights.
A belt that holds half of our dreams,
It's there to keep our pants just right.

Old boots may creak a funky tune,
When worn on dance floors late at night.
They stomp the ground with joy so loud,
Making every mishap feel just right.

A handbag draped on arms like wings,
Whispers of trips and silly thrills.
With pockets deep, it steals our things,
And maybe just a few more bills.

So let's applaud this wondrous stuff,
That brings us giggles day by day.
The threads that connect us through the rough,
In every fold, a laugh at play.

Embrace of the Hide

In jackets snug, we dance with glee,
With every twist, it shouts, "Look at me!"
A squeak, a pop, oh what a sound,
In this soft embrace, joy is found.

Pockets stuffed with snacks galore,
Beware, dear friend, of the hidden score!
A crumb may slip, a treat may fall,
But fashion says, it's worth it all!

A boot that shines with polished pride,
A swagger that can't be denied.
With every step, a little jig,
Who knew foot fashion could be so big!

So let us sport these hides so fine,
With humor tucked in every line.
From clunky shoes to bags so bright,
We'll strut our stuff from morn till night.

Elegance in Every Fold

A handbag clasped, a poise so grand,
It whispers tales of a far-off land.
With every crease, a story told,
Of adventures bold, both hot and cold.

Purses that giggle with a little shake,
When dropped on floors, oh what a quake!
Bags that hold secrets, snacks, and dreams,
Dancing along the style extremes.

Jackets with pockets, just like a child,
Hiding snacks that drive you wild.
A chocolate bar? I'll save it for later,
This chic life does need a few greater skaters!

Folds that catch the morning light,
Strutting down the street, what a sight!
With laughter and whimsy in every thread,
In elegance we live, and wobble instead.

Stories Etched in Grain

Worn and weathered, like old friends,
Each little scratch, a tale that bends.
From wild nights out to quiet chats,
Each mark a journey with silly spats.

Bags that stretch to hold our dreams,
Or maybe just lunch—or so it seems!
With every dent and every tear,
Our fabric friends are always there.

In polished hues and rustic schemes,
They cradle stories like lovely dreams.
But watch out for the clumsy trip,
You'll learn that flaws can really flip!

So let's embrace each stylish trace,
The funny missteps in this wild race.
With laughter ringing through the wear,
These stories etched, we gladly share.

Silhouettes of Softness

A couch that hugs with leather grace,
Where comfy naps find their own place.
With a cat that claims it, royal decree,
It's a throne for two—a sight to see!

A wallet that munches on dollar bills,
Oh dear wallet, please, spare the chills!
Your leather's soft, but money's tight,
Let's budget now, and have some light.

Shoes that dance on wooden floors,
Kicking up giggles, always scores.
With every slide, the laughter's ripe,
In soft silhouettes, we learn to type.

So here's to the tales that leather weaves,
With every fold, it pleads, "Believe!"
In this amusing, stylish spree,
Life's fun with leather—don't you agree?

Affection in Every Stitch

In a shop where fashion dreams shimmer,
A jacket whispers tales of a glimmer.
Hugs wrapped in leather, snug and neat,
Dancing with warmth, oh what a treat!

Pockets that hold both snacks and pride,
Zippers that grin, they won't ever hide.
Mending old seams, like patching a heart,
Each little stitch plays its quirky part.

Worn with a smile, it tells all the jokes,
Stiff at the start, now it laughs with folks.
Every crease and fold, a story profound,
In the world of fabric, it wears the crown.

So wear it with flair, let your humor fly,
With every twirl and spin, you'll surely defy.
In a world of denim, this shines so bright,
A treasure so fun, it's love at first sight!

Color and Character Unfolded

Brown like chocolate, oh what a sight,
The colors of joy that feel just right.
A pop of red, it's daring and bold,
Spilling secrets of laughter untold.

From midnight black to sunny yellow,
Each hue is sassy, each stitch a fellow.
They dance in the closet, a vibrant crew,
Giving life to the outfit that's always new.

Shiny or matte, they play in the light,
A bumpy ride makes everything bright.
The cat thinks it's a scratch pad, oh how sweet,
Leather's our humor, soft yet elite.

In a world of textures, it stands apart,
Oozing with character, it captures the heart.
Each color a chuckle, a shade that winks,
In this playful style, the leather thinks!

Landscapes Crafted in Texture

Rucksacks and belts with stories to share,
Crafted by hands that show love and care.
A journey built strong from the ground to the skies,
Each scuff and scar, a tale that flies.

The wild adventures we take along,
Every trip and tumble has made it strong.
Mountains climbed, and mud splashed on too,
A rugged companion, through and through.

Fields of laughter, and puddles of fun,
We wrangle through life, together as one.
A patch of grass or a cobblestone square,
With every adventure, it's always there.

Years of travel, and still looking fine,
Crumpled maps in pockets, they intertwine.
With every crease, we've made our own art,
In this crafted texture, we find our heart!

Rustle of Journey's Footsteps

A soft rustle follows, what could it be?
It's just my old boots, now they're so free.
They squeak a tune, with every step taken,
Along a path where dreams are awakened.

Through cities and beaches, oh what a sight,
They hold all my secrets, both day and night.
With every stomp, they dance to a beat,
Giving life to my travels, oh what a feat!

Worn from adventures, they're never shy,
They wink at the river, wave at the sky.
Even when muddy, they're always in style,
Join me on journeys, let's go that extra mile!

So here's to the rustle, the joy in my stride,
With each step we take, let laughter be wide.
The tales that they tell, oh what a delight,
In the journey of life, they're my shoes of light!

Soul of the Earth

In a shop filled with odd, squeaky noise,
Lurks a jacket with charm, oh what a poise!
It rides on a chair, with a grin oh-so-wide,
Claiming it's mighty, no need for a ride.

In sunlight it glistens, a sight oh so grand,
But throw it in mud, and it'll make a stand!
With patches of stories, it tells every tale,
Of adventures and mishaps, of coffee and ale.

The wallet's much sneaky, it plays hide and seek,
It gobbles up bills as it gushes with cheek.
"Oh where did you go?" with a wink it replies,
"Check under the couch, you're not that wise!"

A belt with a buckle that gleams like a star,
Holds up all the pants that have traveled so far.
It laughs at the diet, and booms, "You'll be back!"
With a twist and a turn, it keeps up the act!

Gnarled Whisper

Upon a dusty rack, a satchel does sigh,
It dreams of the skies, while resting nearby.
With whispers of journeys, it flutters with glee,
"Did I mention I once flew with a bee?"

A pair of old boots, with stories to share,
They danced through the puddles, caught wind in the air.
"Remember the cha-cha? We stole all the show!"
As they leap off the shelf, putting on quite a show.

A quirky keychain, shaped like a dog,
Holds secrets of laughter, it's never a slog.
With a jingle and jiggle, it chimes when you trip,
"Oh dear, look at you, went and slipped on your lip!"

In corners lies leather, both vintage and bright,
It chuckles and murmurs, "Oh, what a delight!"
Beneath all the dust, friends old and new stand,
Sharing a giggle, they form a wild band!

Tapestry of Textures

Funky old fragments stitched into a dance,
A quilt of soft textures, come join in the chance!
With zippers and buckles, and knots full of cheer,
This patchwork creation, brings smiles ear to ear.

Glove on the shelf, with a grin and a wink,
"You need a partner? Well, pour me a drink!"
It's ready to groove, to the beat of the night,
With fingers a-tapping, oh what a delight!

A cap with a brim, that defies gravity,
Claims it can fly, and brings joy, what a rarity!
Its brim guards the secrets of laughter and fun,
"Join me for shenanigans, we've only begun!"

In pockets of history, lies laughter and hue,
A treasure of memories, for me and for you.
Through ups and through downs, a whimsical saga,
With leather and laughter, oh what a raga!

Poise of the Past

A suitcase with stories, all battered and bruised,
Wanders through time, feeling slightly confused.
It grumbles of travels, of cramped airplane seats,
And the time it got lost in some wayward fleet.

A quirky old purse, with a chain that jingles,
It scoffs at the trends, while its charm still wriggles.
"Oh darling," it giggles, "I've seen it all here,
Fashion's a circle; let's raise up a cheer!"

A lovably odd chair, with cushions so worn,
Sits proudly in corners, like it's just been reborn.
"Sit down and relax, let your troubles go free,
I promise this spot is the best place to be!"

A trunk full of leather, both vibrant and frayed,
It beams with the joy of the lives it conveyed.
In laughter's embrace, through thick and through thin,
This poise of the past, is forever our kin!

The Language of Touch

In a shop with lots of flair,
I spotted boots with a unique air.
They whispered secrets, soft and bold,
A tale of journeys yet untold.

I tried them on, a perfect fit,
The squeak it made was quite a hit.
Each step a giggle, each turn a dance,
In shoes that made me take a chance.

The texture tells of days gone by,
A leather patch for each little sigh.
Oh, the memories they might conceal,
Like hiding chocolate, oh, what a steal!

So here I stand, with flair and glee,
This silly world of leather, see?
A merry game of tactile bliss,
In every stitch, a dreamy kiss.

Tides of Tradition

From granddad's chair to dad's old shoes,
In classic hues, what could I choose?
Each wrinkle knows of laughter shared,
Tales of the family love declared.

With every scuff and scratch, a mark,
A journey etched, like a cheerful lark.
Old belts that once held up the pants,
Now dance around, in random prance!

A wallet stuffed with cards galore,
It holds my dreams, and maybe more.
Each pocket filled with tales so grand,
In a bundle held within my hand.

In this sea of endless glee,
Tradition flows, like waves set free.
With leather's grace, I can't resist,
The fun of life, a leather twist!

Isolated Fragrance

Oh, the scent that fills the air,
From wallets and shoes, without a care.
A whiff of spice, a dash of glee,
What secrets hide in this odyssey?

In shops where quality's the game,
Each piece distinct, never the same.
Like a sneeze that blooms in spring,
In every bag, joy takes wing.

I catch a drift of history's past,
With laughs and quirks, these treasures last.
The leather sings a funny tune,
A dance beneath the dappled moon.

I sniff my jacket, what a find!
It smells like stories left behind.
In this embrace, I find the art,
Of laughing scents, that touch the heart.

Richness of Ruins

In an old attic, dust and cheer,
I stumbled on boots, with quite a leer.
Their tales of wandering far and wide,
Promised adventures in every stride.

A faded jacket, with sass of style,
Worn by a grandpa, who loved a smile.
His leather belt, a twist of fate,
Tells of stories that wouldn't wait.

The fashion sense is quite absurd,
In these relics of a world unheard.
I wear them proud, like a clown in town,
With every layer, I never frown.

So here I stand, a quirky muse,
In garments rich, with nothing to lose.
Unearthed treasures, oh what a scoop,
In leather's clutches, I form a troop!

Whispers of Tanned Hide

In a shop of oddities, I did find,
A jacket that giggled, one of a kind.
It swayed with a rhythm, a dance all its own,
Claiming it whispered, 'Take me, you're grown!'

But as I slipped on that quirky delight,
It shrieked with laughter, a comical sight.
Friends gathered 'round with riotous cheer,
'Is that you or the jacket we hear?'

With cunning charisma, it took to the floor,
A star on display, begging for more.
Yet every dance move, a squeak came alive,
The leather had learned how to jive and thrive!

From tanned creations, a character true,
They taught me the charm of a giggle or two.
So next time you spot leather at play,
Remember to listen, it might have its say!

Midnight Embrace of Buckskin

In the moonlight, buckskin does glow,
It wrapped me up tight, 'til I couldn't say no.
I tripped and I stumbled, a tumble and roll,
That leather was laughing, 'You're losing control!'

A midnight caper, with flaps flapping wide,
This buckskin's embrace was quite difficult to hide.
'Hold on,' it chuckled, 'we've miles to explore!'
But silly old me, ended up at a store!

I tried to steal glances, in mirrors and glass,
While passing onlookers just watched as I pass.
'Is that a new style? Do you dare to wear,'
Buckskin chimed in, 'just ignore all the stares!'

With each shrill cackle, I reveled in glee,
This midnight caper was fun as can be.
So when I look back on that whimsical night,
I'll cherish the laughter and moonbeams so bright!

Elegance Woven in Layers

Layers of elegance, stitched with delight,
Hanging in closets, oh what a sight!
But under the glamour, there's mischief in store,
A jacket that giggles and can't help but roar!

It whispers sweet nothings and tells silly tales,
Of being a hero as a pirate with sails.
Yet when the doorbell rings, it falls flat,
Dramatic and bold, or just a poor cat?

Among the fine fabrics, it laughs like a fool,
A fine roguish creature defying the rule.
With skirts that may twirl and jackets that sway,
That humor in leather just makes my day!

So wear it with pride when you step out the door,
Dare to embrace every laugh and encore.
For elegance shines, not just in the seams,
But in giggles and ripples, and wonderfully dreams!

Notes of a Well-Worn Journal

Oh, the stories tucked inside old leather binds,
Pages filled with laughter, mischief entwined.
Each scribbled note holds a fragment of glee,
Like squirrels with nut stashes, just wild and free!

Underneath the cover, wisdom may dwell,
But don't let it fool you, it's all in the shell.
Mistakes make great tales, much better than wealth,
Quirky adventures in the book of oneself!

A saucy confession, I penned late one night,
How I danced like a fool at the wrong party light.
I laughed with a grin, secretly wishing it true,
That all of life's blunders would bring laughter too!

So here's to the journals with their crinkled pages,
They hold more than secrets from all of the stages.
For leather, my friend, has a humor it brings,
Tales of our lives woven in joys and in flings!

Stories Buried in Scent

In dusty shops where treasures lie,
A jacket whispers tales nearby.
It smells of mischief, laughs galore,
And sneaky adventures from days of yore.

Pockets stuffed with gum and fluff,
This old bag's seen more than enough.
Yet every scuff, a badge of pride,
In sticky situations, it's our guide.

The aroma swirls, a mystery dance,
Each scratch and mark, a funny chance.
Who knew a belt could share a plot?
Each fold a story, forgotten but hot.

So if you smell this leather treat,
Imagine the places it's been on its feet.
From wild disco nights to rainy day fun,
The stories unfold, we laugh and run.

Resilience Wrapped in Elegance

A purse so prim, so chic it seems,
Yet hides the snacks of midnight dreams.
With crumpled notes and gum stuck tight,
Its elegance boasts, 'I am alright!'

Jackets that wrinkle, a fine old grace,
Worn with pride despite the race.
Every wrinkle's a tale, a journey grand,
From 'who wore it best?' to 'was that planned?'

An old shoe grins, a true charmer still,
Though covered in mud, it has the thrill.
Dance floors and puddles, it's seen it through,
With tap-tap-taps, it knows just what to do.

So let's toast to wear, to each little tear,
For resilience wrapped in laughter, we share.
In funny mishaps, we twirl and sway,
Elegance dressed in the light of day.

Symphonies of Wear and Tear

In the corner sits a chair so fine,
With squeaks and groans like an old shoelace line.
It sings of tales as it rocks away,
Of cats who leaped and kids at play.

The sole of a boot hums an old tune,
As it stumbles along, under a bright moon.
Each scuff a note in its raucous score,
A symphony made for laughter and more.

Belts that stretch and buckle with glee,
Remind us all of holiday spree.
They hold us tight as we bite into cake,
And stretch just enough, make no mistake!

So here's to the laughter from wear and tear,
In every piece, a moment to share.
With funny old notes and a laugh that rings,
The chorus of life in leather sings.

Comfort Found in Weight

A handbag so heavy, it could take flight,
But inside it holds my snacks, what a sight!
With lip balms, keys, and a sandwich maybe,
It's the bag that says, 'Hey! I'm your baby!'

Boots that stomp and feel like home,
With every step, I comfortably roam.
Though they may squeak when I hop and see,
My trusty companions, they dance with me.

A satchel slouches, sagging with pride,
Belly full of memories, it's a wild ride.
With each awkward wiggle and gentle sway,
It laughs at the world, come what may.

So embrace the heft, the weight of the fun,
In all our bundles, adventures begun.
Through laughter and comfort, we wander and play,
Finding joy in the heft of the everyday.